Inside Special Operations

SAS

British Special
Air Service

WHO DARES WINS

Amanda Ferguson

the rosen publishing group's
rosen central

Published in 2003 by The Rosen Publishing Group, Inc.
29 East 21st Street, New York, NY 10010

Library of Congress Cataloging-in-Publication Data

Ferguson, Amanda.
SAS : British special air service / by Amanda Ferguson.— 1st ed.
    p. cm.—(inside special operations)
Summary: A look at Britain's special operations force, the SAS, including information on its creation and history, selection and training, uniforms, equipment, and current operations.
Includes bibliographical references and index.
ISBN 0-8239-3810-7 (library binding)
1. Great Britain. Army. Special Air Service—Juvenile literature. 2. Special forces (Military science)—Great Britain—History—Juvenile literature. 3. Great Britain. Army—Commando troops—History—Juvenile literature. [1. Great Britain. Army. Special Air Service. 2. Special forces (Military science)—Great Britain—History.] I. Title.
UA659.S67 F47 2003
356'.1673'0941—dc21
                                                                                2002007771

Manufactured in the United States of America

Contents

Introduction   5

1 The Birth of the SAS   10

2 A Shift in Tactics   18

3 Post–World War II   24

4 Selection   34

5 Training and Equipment   40

6 The Present and Future of the SAS   48

Glossary   56
For More Information   58
For Further Reading   59
Bibliography   60
Index   62

SAS members work with U.S. Special Forces in the Tornak Farms camp outside Kandahar Airport in Afghanistan. The Al Qaeda training camp was bombed by the United States and its allies in response to the September 11, 2001, terrorist attacks. Special forces units cleared debris and searched the area for mines and unexploded mortars.

Introduction

On Wednesday, April 30, 1980, at 11:25 AM, six men walked up to a terraced house just off Hyde Park, a residential neighborhood in London. The men were terrorists, and the white, five-story building was the Iranian Embassy. The men were dressed in checkered scarves and anoraks and carried duffel bags filled with weapons: three Browning self-loading pistols, a .38 revolver, ammunition, and five Russian hand grenades. Two of the men had submachine guns hidden under their anoraks. The men were obviously not on a diplomatic mission.

The main doors of the embassy were open. Trevor Lock, a security guard who worked for the

Diplomatic Protection Group, stood in the lobby. One of the terrorists grabbed Lock. Lock managed to kick the outer door shut, but another terrorist fired three shots through the glass panel. The men forced their way inside. One of the terrorists fired a round from his automatic machine gun into the ceiling. A few people inside the embassy were quick enough to escape. Two men escaped out a back window; another climbed out a fourth floor window into an adjoining building. When the terrorists had secured the building, twenty-six embassy staff and visitors were held captive.

The terrorists issued demands. They said that if their demands were met, no one would be hurt. Otherwise, hostages would be killed. Before he was taken hostage, Lock managed to radio an alert. Police were on the scene almost immediately. While they tried to negotiate with the terrorists, the entire area was sealed off by specialist units, including police marksmen and antiterrorist officers. At 11:48 AM, the beepers of a special military regiment sounded. A squadron of the Special Air Service (SAS) was called together for a briefing and asked to stand by.

This was not the first time that the SAS, a special forces military unit, had been asked to help counter terrorists. When a Palestinian terrorist group killed eleven Israeli athletes at the 1972 Munich Olympics, European governments realized that they needed forces capable of dealing with such atrocities. In Britain, the SAS was asked to prepare an antiterrorist force. The regiment built the Killing House, where SAS troopers practiced dealing with hostage crises. The men were trained to detect and kill enemies without injuring hostages. Different rooms were constructed to help SAS troopers practice for real-life situations. One room was made to look like the interior of an airplane so troopers could see what it might be like to rescue a hijacked aircraft.

When the call came in about the crisis at the Iranian Embassy, the SAS counterterrorist team had been in action only three times. The British government ordered police to negotiate a peaceful solution with the terrorists. Police could use force only if it was clear that hostages were being killed. Over the next six days, the terrorists grew increasingly frustrated with negotiations. The terrorists' spokesperson warned that hostages would be shot. On the afternoon of May 5, three shots were heard. A few hours later, another group of shots rang out. The front door of the embassy was opened just wide enough for the terrorists to dump out a body. When police retrieved the body, they could see that the man had been dead for several hours. This meant that a second person might also be dead. The SAS was given permission for an assault, code-named Operation Nimrod.

As terrorists held twenty-six people hostage inside the Iranian Embassy in London, SAS operatives devised a plan to free the hostages. In a showdown that lasted just over ten minutes, the SAS fired tear gas into the building and stormed the rooms where the hostages were held.

The SAS divided into two teams, each operating in two-man units. One team climbed on top of the embassy roof with abseiling (rappelling) equipment. The other team prepared charges to blow out the windows and gain entry. Neither team was sure where the hostages and terrorists were located. One abseiler got stuck dangling above the balcony when his ropes got tangled. When his partner tried to free him, the trooper's boot knocked against a window. The noise alerted the terrorists, so the SAS began its assault.

The team in charge of explosives set off charges to disorient the terrorists while those on the other team lowered themselves into the building. The sound of the explosions could be heard from miles away. Next, SAS troopers blew out the windows and poured into the building. They threw stun grenades and tear gas and began moving though the embassy. SAS troopers ordered hostages to get out of the way as they shot the terrorists' spokesperson. Another terrorist was shot and killed before he could use his weapon. A couple of the other terrorists threw down their weapons when they heard the SAS. They tried to hide among the hostages. SAS troopers asked the hostages to identify the terrorists and then shot them dead.

Two terrorists were still unaccounted for. The SAS passed the remaining hostages down the stairs through a human chain. They found one terrorist and shot him dead. The last terrorist was found hiding among the hostages. He was the only terrorist to survive. The only casualty among the hostages had been the man shot earlier. The second shooting had proven to be a bluff.

From start to finish, the entire operation took eleven minutes. Those watching the events on live television knew nothing about the mysterious black-clad figures swarming over and into the embassy. Only when the assault was over did the public learn that the mission had been carried out by the SAS. In a matter of minutes, the members of the SAS had become national celebrities. In truth, the SAS had been carrying out high-risk special missions for decades.

1. The Birth of the SAS

In 1933, Adolf Hitler was made German chancellor. He quickly established himself as dictator. Hitler built up the German military and signed treaties with Italy and Japan, creating an alliance of powers that came to be known as the Axis.

True to his political promises, Hitler began an aggressive expansion campaign. In March 1938, Germany annexed Austria. In September, Germany annexed a piece of land on the western border of Czechoslovakia, home of many ethnic Germans. Six months later, in March 1939, Germany took the remainder of Czechoslovakia. On

September 1, 1939, German armies marched into Poland. The German army seemed intent on conquering mainland Europe. Two days later, Britain and France declared war on Germany.

By the time Britain and France (the Allied forces) entered the war, they were at a disadvantage. The Germans had perfected a military technique called the Blitzkrieg, or "lightening war," which caught western Europe off guard. British commanders expected the kind of battles that had been fought in the trenches during World War I. Instead, a barrage of German tanks, guns, and dive-bombers smashed their way through Allied resistance. In June 1940, France signed an armistice with Germany. Britain felt alone in facing the threat of a German invasion. To make matters worse, many of Britain's military divisions were short of equipment and had no transport.

On September 1, 1939, London's *Evening Standard* announced the German invasion of Poland, which started World War II. The SAS was born from the need to fight the overwhelming power of Germany's Blitzkriegs.

The Founders of the SAS: Jock Lewes and David Stirling

David Stirling was the mastermind behind the organization of the first SAS unit, then known as L Detachment. He is often credited with originating the SAS motto, "Who Dares Wins."

Although most of the fighting took place in mainland Europe, Britain stationed troops in North Africa and Greece to protect these strategic areas against German and Italian invasions. One such British force, the Commando Layforce ("L"), was largely inactive in 1941. Two members of Britain's Commando L, Jock Lewes and Commanding Officer David Stirling, used their free time to develop a plan to attack the enemy using very few resources. After taking part in and witnessing many failed operations, Lewes became impatient. He thought that the methods and training of the commandos were insufficient. He thought that the commando units were too large and unorganized to perform well.

He thought that raiding operations would be successful only if carried out by a small, highly trained force. He discussed his ideas with Stirling, who agreed with some of the points that Lewes made.

An accidental shipment of parachutes caught Lewes's attention. Lewes thought that the parachutes could be used to drop soldiers behind enemy lines. Soldiers could then collect intelligence, conduct raids, and create havoc. He asked his commander if he could create his own small parachuting force to operate behind enemy lines. Lewes got permission to detach a small section from the unit and train it to perform an operation that he had planned.

The operation was postponed three times. Meanwhile, the men, none of whom had ever jumped before, made trial jumps. On one of these jumps, Stirling was badly injured when his chute caught on the tail of the plane and ripped. His spine was damaged, and he also lost his eyesight for a short period. In the end, due to a lack of decision among top officials, Lewes's operation was never carried out.

The Proposal

Disappointed, Lewes and a few men from Commando Layforce were sent to Tobruk, a port on the coast of North Africa in Libya, where Lewes established himself as a top patrol commander. The rest of the commando disbanded. Meanwhile, Stirling recovered in a hospital in Alexandria, Egypt. Stirling used this time to study the desert war. News from the front was bad. German troops, under the command of General Marshal Erwin Rommel, were at the Egyptian border. A number of raids against Rommel's communication lines had failed.

Stirling decided to use his contacts with military officials to promote Lewes's ideas about a small special forces unit. He wrote a proposal and presented it to Britain's Middle Eastern headquarters. He argued that the British military operations lacked an element of surprise. He thought small subunits of highly trained men could carry out some missions that larger forces of 200 men could not. Small raiding units could ambush the enemy while conserving men, supplies, and equipment.

Stirling was promoted to captain and given permission to recruit six officers and sixty men for a new unit. Based in Kabrit, Egypt, near the Suez Canal, Stirling's new force was known as L Detachment, Special Air Service Brigade. (In fact, there was no such brigade. A brigadier named Dudley Clark came up with the name to convince the enemy that Britain had a powerful, new air force in Africa.)

The first officer Stirling applied for was Lewes. Lewes brought four men who had served with him in Tobruk.

Other recruits were volunteers from the old commando force. If Lewes resented Stirling for commanding the unit that he had thought of, he showed no signs of it. Lewes was dedicated and enthusiastic, and the two men worked well together. While Stirling worked on getting supplies and official approvals, Lewes created an intensive three-month training program to shape the first SAS units.

New Training, New Strategies

Although there was an official hierarchy, SAS soldiers and officers often worked side by side. All men were expected to respect and learn from one another's skills. Men received equal training in navigation, weapons, explosives, intelligence gathering, medical care, and vehicle operation, including that of planes. Members of the SAS had to be prepared for any situation. They had to be in excellent shape in case they needed to march long distances in short periods of time. They were expected to work their way up to covering 95 miles (approximately 153 kilometers) in three days. The men played blindman's bluff in order to develop sensitivity in the dark. They went on treasure hunts to improve their resourcefulness. These games helped soldiers to develop important military skills and kept the difficult training more pleasurable.

Lewes thought that small-scale raids would be effective against the German airfields along the North African coast. He thought the fields, which had no fences and were relatively unguarded, would be easy targets. Because the SAS khaki uniforms were similar to Italian and German uniforms, Lewes thought that the SAS could slip into the airfields fairly easily. But he worried that individual parachutists would not be able to carry enough ammunition to destroy aircraft.

While the SAS trained, Lewes spent his spare time inventing a lightweight bomb that could be easily carried and activated. In his makeshift lab, Lewes developed bombs that could be shaped into tennis ball-sized explosives. These came to be known as Lewes bombs, or sticky bombs. A captain from Britain's Royal Air Force came to evaluate the SAS's chances of successfully raiding an airfield. The officer was impressed by the SAS's capabilities, and in November 1941, the SAS was given its first mission.

The First Operation

The plan was to hit five enemy airfields on the North African coast. The SAS would blow up enemy aircraft, paving the way for a larger British military offensive. On November 16, 1941, five aged Bristol Bombay aircraft took off to drop five SAS units near their targets despite terrible desert winds. After two hours, the planes reached their targets. The planes came under attack. One plane was shot down, killing the crew and one soldier; survivors were taken prisoner. A second aircraft vanished. No one knew whether the plane had crashed or was shot down. The three remaining units jumped into strong, gale-force winds. Their landmarks were destroyed in a sandstorm, so the men did not know where to land. Supplies went missing. Men were badly injured. They found their bombs but no detonators. Without detonators, the men could not carry out the mission. Only twenty-two out of the sixty-five men dropped made it back to the rendezvous. The mission was a complete disaster.

2. A Shift in Tactics

Things were not going well for Britain's North African counteroffensive against Germany. Supplies were low. The German army had crossed into Egypt. Down to twenty-six men, Stirling withdrew the remainder of his troops to a remote oasis while he rethought his strategy.

Dropping SAS troopers by parachute had proven unreliable at best, disastrous at worst. However, their pickup by the Long Range Desert Group (LRDG), a British unit that ran intelligence operations behind enemy lines, went off without a hitch. Lewes thought that if the LRDG could pick up SAS troopers, the LRDG could also drop them off. Stirling asked officials if the LRDG could be used to drop the SAS within walking distance of their targets. The LRDG agreed. With the LRDG's help, the SAS was able to carry out a string of successful missions.

The LRDG were able to transport SAS troopers far behind enemy lines, dropping them off to raid supply and equipment centers. Before long, SAS patrols were in action every night, shooting at enemy camps and ambushing enemy vehicles. They surprised the enemy with short bursts of destruction. In December 1941, a small unit of SAS "originals" (original SAS members) launched successful attacks against enemy airfields along the North African coast. More than 100 aircraft along with stores of fuel and vehicles were destroyed.

These Men Are Dangerous

The raids carried out by the SAS were very effective. Every destroyed piece of equipment and supply store created new burdens for their enemies. After the first flurry of action, the SAS kept up attacks at a steady pace. The SAS developed a highly regarded reputation. In his field notes, German general Erwin Rommel noted that the SAS attacks "seriously disquieted the Italians." The enemy was determined to hunt down SAS and LRDG patrols. In his memoir, *These Men Are Dangerous*,

CLOSE-UP

Legend has it that Jock Lewes (below) designed the parachute wings that are worn on the right shoulder of SAS soldiers. A more forceful invention was the Lewes bomb, a one-pound device that could be carried in bulk by soldiers to provide maximum damage.

former SAS trooper Derrick Harrison notes that Hitler himself viewed the SAS as a major threat, commanding that the "highly dangerous" SAS be handed over to the nearest Gestapo unit and "ruthlessly exterminated."

The Loss of One of Its Founders

After the SAS returned to the base following a successful raid on Nofilia, the North African airfield, German fighter aircraft troops spotted and attacked the unit. Lewes was hit by a cannon shell, and a main artery in his leg was severed. Though Lewes received immediate medical attention, he died fifteen minutes later. The remaining troops were forced to disperse.

Despite the loss, the SAS conducted more successful raids. In early 1942, the future of the SAS seemed assured. Stirling is given credit for designing the unit's official insignia, a winged dagger badge to be worn on a beret. The colors of the new insignia were dark blue and light blue, reflecting Stirling's Oxford and Lewes's Cambridge rowing backgrounds. Some sources say that Stirling composed the official motto; others say it was Lewes. Regardless, "Who Dares Wins" remains the SAS motto to this day.

In January 1943, Stirling was captured by German soldiers while sleeping in a cave. He escaped the same day, but the people he took shelter with turned him in. Stirling spent the rest of the war in captivity. In his field notes, Erwin Rommel recalled Stirling's capture: "Insufficiently guarded, he managed to escape and made his way to some Arabs, to whom he offered a reward if they would get him back to the British lines. But his bid must have been too small, for the Arabs . . . offered him to us for 5 kg of tea—a bargain which we soon clinched. Thus the British lost the very able and adaptable commander of the desert group which had caused us more damage than any other British unit of equal strength."

After Stirling's capture, the SAS split into two forces. The original force, led by Blair "Paddy" Mayne, was called the Special Raiding Squadron (SRS). The second force, led by Stirling's brother, William, was called the 2nd SAS.

Members of the Long Range Desert Group (LRDG). An intelligence-gathering reconnaissance unit, the LRDG was the idea of Major Ralph Bagnold, Royal Signal Corps. The SAS joined forces with the LRDG, using their vehicles to transport SAS troopers behind enemy lines.

In May 1943, Axis forces in North Africa surrendered. The Allied North African campaign was officially over. But the SAS was not out of action for long. When Allied forces invaded Sicily, Italy, the SAS was called in to assist. The SRS attacked Germans landing in Sicily in July 1943. They moved behind enemy lines to disrupt German and Italian coastal bases in the Balkans and central Mediterranean. At the same time, the 2nd SAS force dropped behind enemy lines to conduct raids and to provide intelligence in support of Allied landings. They destroyed bridges, hit airfields, and helped to coordinate the efforts of resistance groups.

In 1944, both SAS groups prepared for the Allied invasion of northwest Europe. The troops worked together with the French resistance, training and organizing them in an effort to drive the Germans out of France. When the Germans left France, the SAS helped Allied forces to cross the Rhine River for the final defeat of German armies. They helped civilians to accept the surrender. The last major SAS operation was to gather German soldiers in Norway and help them to return to Germany.

In April 1945, David Stirling was released from captivity. He returned to England, where he presented a detailed plan for the SAS to continue their operations against Axis forces in the Far East. The plan was approved by Prime Minister Winston Churchill, but before SAS troops were deployed, the war ended. Japan had surrendered. World War II was over. The future of the SAS was uncertain.

3. Post-World War II

Though the SAS was disbanded after the war, some members were sent on various reconnaissance, or fact-finding, missions to find out what happened to thirty-two missing SAS soldiers. The missing soldiers were last seen in October 1944, after they were deployed on a mission in Alsace, France. It was reported that the men had been captured and executed by the Germans.

A six-man team commanded by Major Eric Barkworth set off from England to Germany. The team's mission was to find and identify the missing bodies. After six months, the team had accounted for each of the missing men. The group also tracked down the men responsible for killing the SAS troopers. These men were arrested and hanged.

When this mission was completed, it seemed that the work of the SAS was officially finished. However, a few former SAS members did not want the unit to disband. They lobbied Britain's War Office, and in 1947, an SAS unit was formed within the territorial army. This unit was known as the 21st SAS. It included many wartime members as well as part-time reserve soldiers.

Military Actions

In the two decades following World War II, the British government withdrew from its former colonies. The bulk of colonies in the former British Empire, including Burma, Palestine, the Nile Delta, Aden, Cyprus, Malta, India, Kenya, Uganda, and Nigeria, switched from colonial rule to independence.

An SAS officer instructing his men during an exercise in 1947. After WWII, the SAS was disbanded but was resurrected in 1947 as the 21st SAS. The SAS continues to operate under a great cloak of secrecy.

Not all of these transitions of power were easy. Many rebel groups looked to challenge the new governments. While Britain no longer held direct power in these new national governments, it still wanted to have a say about who would be in power.

It didn't take long for the British government to recognize the merits of maintaining the small, specialist military team skilled in the art of fighting rebels in deserts, jungles, and mountains. In 1960, a regular Special Air Service formation, 22nd SAS, moved to permanent base at Hereford, England, where it remains today. The SAS is made up of four squadrons. Three of these are available for covert political and military missions around the world. One squadron remains in Britain in case of a threat at home.

Because the SAS usually operates in secret, many details of its operations are unknown to the public. Still, various former SAS members have written about their experiences, and on occasion, SAS operations make the newspapers and history books. While Britain has not been officially involved in an all-out war since World War II, it has been involved in several military actions, including counterinsurgency operations and antiterrorist missions. The SAS has been in active duty for more than sixty years, from the Malayan jungles to the Irish countryside.

Men from the 22nd SAS Regiment carry an injured member to a helicopter for evacuation during fighting in Malaya. The Malayan Emergency (1948–1960) was a full-scale war between the Malayan Communist Party (MCP) and the British and Malayan authorities.

Malaya

In 1948, an uprising began in Malaya that would last for more than a decade. The Malayan Emergency, as it became known, started when a group of communist revolutionaries made a series of attacks against the recently formed Federation of Malay. The communists would come out of the jungle, kill police and civilians, and run back to their hideouts. The regular Malayan army had trouble rooting out these invaders. They asked Britain for help. Britain tried to control the uprising with roadblocks and guarded convoys, but these methods had little impact.

Mike Calvert, a soldier who had commanded the SAS brigade during its last World War II missions in Europe, was asked to analyze the Malayan problem. He proposed that a special force be formed that could live, work, and fight in the jungle. This force would be able to watch and wait for the right opportunity to ambush the enemy. Calvert's plan was approved. In 1950, troops from the 21st SAS, dubbed the Malayan Scouts, were sent to Malaya. In 1952, the Malayan Scouts became the 22nd Special Air Service Regiment. The 22nd SAS fought the Malayan communists until the group was finally suppressed in 1959.

In 1963, SAS troops were again sent to the region, this time to protect the Federation of Malaya against the Indonesian government under President Sukarno, who wanted to add territory to his empire. Limited to volunteers, the SAS was split into three- and four-man teams. Each man had his own specialty. Training was difficult and unorthodox. The jungle was full of hazards, including disease, poisonous reptiles, and dangerous vegetation. Because the SAS did not have enough men to sufficiently seal the Malayan-Indonesian border, diplomacy was their most effective weapon. SAS soldiers needed to count on the local tribes for assistance, especially for information about the enemy. Soldiers gained the trust and help of natives by talking to them, providing medical assistance, and making social visits. The confrontation came to an end when a new regime seized power in Indonesia. SAS troops were withdrawn in 1966.

Women in the SAS

While there are no female members in the main core of the SAS, one British special forces community recruits women on an equal basis with men: The 14th Intelligence Company. The 14th Intelligence Company is often referred to as "the Det" because it is split into so many detachments. This highly select unit was formed in 1974, a combination of SAS members, Intelligence Corp. surveillance specialists, and select infantry volunteers. The unit was sent to the most hostile parts of Northern Ireland to collect information about terrorists.

Female members of the Det go through the same SAS training as their male counterparts, with an emphasis on intelligence gathering. In her 1997 memoir, *One Up: A Woman in Action with the SAS*, Det veteran Sarah Ford writes that while she doesn't understand the rules that keep women out of the main branch of the SAS, her work in the Det was dangerous, adventurous, and rewarding.

Northern Ireland

For better and for worse, the SAS is perhaps best known for its role fighting terrorists in Northern Ireland. In 1920, Ireland was granted home rule. However, six counties of the northern province of Ulster wanted to maintain close ties with Great Britain. The region became a separate political division of the United Kingdom called Northern Ireland. The Republic of Ireland hoped that this division would be temporary, but Northern Ireland refused to reunite. A boundary between the two nations was fixed in 1925. Many people in Northern Ireland believe that the boundary preserves their culture and economy. The Republic of Ireland believes that the separation benefits Britain at the expense of the Irish people. 1n 1955, members of the outlawed Irish Republican Army (IRA) began a campaign of terrorism in order to reunite Ireland. These acts were countered by gangs of terrorists who wanted Northern Ireland to remain loyal to Great Britain (loyalists). Both the IRA and loyalist gangs are responsible for serious and frequent acts of terrorism.

Because the SAS works in secret, it is difficult to know exactly how it operates in Northern Ireland. But it is known that the SAS has been involved in ambush and intelligence missions in Ireland since 1969. They maintain hidden sentry posts in rural and urban areas, looking for known terrorists and weapon caches. SAS troopers might infiltrate organizations of known or suspected terrorists in order to learn about their next target. Most sources say that the SAS has a high rate of success, even if the results of their activities are unknown to the general public.

Oman

In 1970, in an operation code-named STORM, the SAS was sent to southern Oman, a nation on the southeast corner of the Arabian Peninsula, to support Oman's ruler against guerrilla attacks. Because the SAS had experience fighting in difficult, desert terrain, the SAS was asked to fight the communist-backed guerrillas and help to train the Omani army. The SAS mainly waged a war of psychology and propaganda against the communists. They gained the support of the local Jebali people by helping them to build wells, schools, clinics, and shops. Eventually, thousands of Iranian and Jordanian troops joined in support of Oman's forces. The combined forces isolated the communist guerrillas and cut off their supplies. The guerrillas were defeated at the end of 1975.

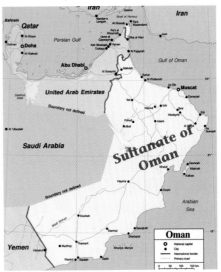

A treaty signed in 1800 states that the friendship between England and Oman should remain "till the end of time, and till the sun and moon have finished their revolving career."

Falkland Islands

The Falkland Islands had been under British rule since 1833. But Argentina had longstanding claims over the islands. In 1982, General Leopoldo Galtiere, leader of Argentina's military junta, decided to reclaim the islands. Galtiere's forces invaded the Falklands. Britain's prime minister Margaret Thatcher resolved to get the islands back, by force if necessary. The SAS volunteered to participate in the campaign. As in World War II, SAS troopers were dropped near or behind enemy lines to gather intelligence and to destroy enemy aircraft.

The SAS raided Pebble Island in the Falklands, destroying more Argentine aircraft than in any air battles. Though Britain achieved victory, it suffered losses as well. In an accident involving a Sea King helicopter, eighteen SAS troopers were killed.

Gulf War

The Gulf War began when Iraqi dictator Saddam Hussein invaded the tiny sheikdom of Kuwait on August 2, 1990. A combination of other nations led by the United States and operating under the United Nations banner set out to expel him. Officially, the response was intended to deter other dictators from similar acts. Most likely, however, the international community wanted to protect and secure the region's vast oil resources. The brief war was fought mainly in the air and with missiles. SAS's exact role remains a mystery, though it is known that they were involved in ground actions behind enemy lines.

Following the Gulf War, the SAS continues to be a presence around the world. They have operated in the former Yugoslavia, trained antinarcotics police in Colombia, hunted ivory poachers in Kenya, and provided instructors at NATO's (the North Atlantic Treaty Organization) special-forces schools. This school helps to train special forces from nations friendly with Britain. With current threats to international security, the SAS is a strong presence in trouble spots around the world.

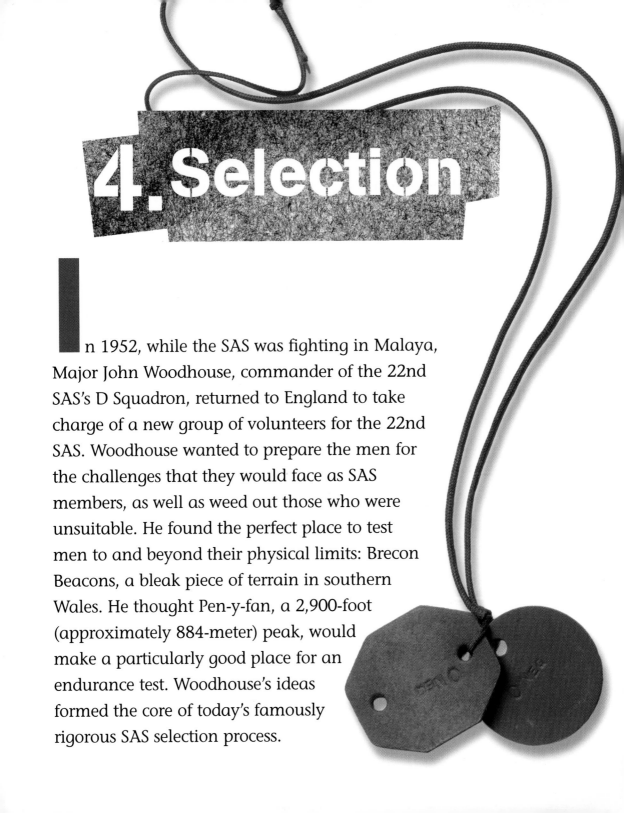

4. Selection

In 1952, while the SAS was fighting in Malaya, Major John Woodhouse, commander of the 22nd SAS's D Squadron, returned to England to take charge of a new group of volunteers for the 22nd SAS. Woodhouse wanted to prepare the men for the challenges that they would face as SAS members, as well as weed out those who were unsuitable. He found the perfect place to test men to and beyond their physical limits: Brecon Beacons, a bleak piece of terrain in southern Wales. He thought Pen-y-fan, a 2,900-foot (approximately 884-meter) peak, would make a particularly good place for an endurance test. Woodhouse's ideas formed the core of today's famously rigorous SAS selection process.

Recruitment

SAS selection is extremely difficult. The selection process ensures that valuable training is spent only on the very best recruits. In the early days, entry into the SAS was voluntary and informal. It was usually a matter of introduction. Recruitment for the 22nd SAS Regiment today is still on a volunteer basis, but selection is much more demanding. SAS trooper Barry Davies recalls that out of the 140 men in his selection course, only 13 were admitted into the SAS.

The SAS is a unit of the British army, and all recruits are drawn from various army units. Even volunteering for the SAS can be an ordeal. Soldiers from one's home unit may view volunteers as thinking too highly of themselves or as traitors. This can be particularly awkward since most volunteers don't make selection and end up RTU—Returned to Unit. Even so, the SAS has a special reputation. Those who make it past the grueling selection process can take pride in knowing that they are in the company of some of the best soldiers in the world.

Any male member of the Royal Army, Navy, or Air Force, or the territorial army is eligible to apply for SAS selection. Officers must be from twenty-two to thirty-four years old. Troopers applying for any other rank must be between the ages of nineteen and thirty-four. All men must have at least three years and three months left to serve from the time when they pass selection.

The SAS wants recruits who are in excellent physical condition. Candidates must train like Olympic athletes. The SAS also looks for disciplined men who can work as a team and follow orders. Men also must be highly independent, able to make decisions and carry them out alone, without direction from a "higher up." They must maintain good judgment and carry out tasks despite mental and physical hardships such as torture, fear, stress, fatigue, isolation, and severe weather conditions.

Selection Tests

Once a soldier has put his name forth as an applicant and has been accepted to go through selection, he undergoes a three-week training and testing period followed by a final week of testing. The process begins with a standard Army Battle Fitness Test followed by daily marches across Brecon Beacons. For the first two weeks, candidates work as a team. On the third week, candidates face challenges alone. In the 1960s, candidates' bergens (knapsacks) were filled with bricks. Today, they are filled with equipment. Among other things, men carry a sleeping mat, a rain poncho, two 1.5-pint water bottles, rations, a self-loading rifle, a standard army compass, and maps. (SAS soldiers almost never write on maps. They also must fold them carefully along their original creases. This is done in case the map is lost. SAS

Sickeners

In the 1970s, it was reported that the SAS designed special challenges, called sickeners, for potential candidates. SAS veteran Peter Scholey recalls a sickener from his selection in Stephen Bull's book, *SAS: Special Forces in Action*:

"Tim had saved up the most challenging ordeal for the end. He lined us up and introduced us to the horrors of the entrails trench: a ditch beside a hawthorn hedge, two feet deep, four feet across, filled with stagnant water and rotting sheep innards . . . I took a deep breath and plunged into the foul mess. Two feet doesn't sound very deep, but when you are crawling on all fours so close to the ground it is very deep . . . Halfway across, weighed down by my bergen, I felt my belt snag on a rock. I couldn't use my hands to free myself as they were holding my rifle clear of the surface. I had to resort to wriggling free by shaking my hips. As I did so . . . the filthy stinking sheep-gut liquid splashed up around my lips. I coughed and spat in disgust."

candidates must be able to memorize a great deal of specific information.) The equipment weighs fifty-five pounds (about twenty-five kilograms) on average.

Marches are scheduled both day and night. Candidates fight the clock and the elements to get to their assigned destinations on time. The men must often go without sleep to reach their rendezvous point on time. Distances and bergen weight are increased daily. The candidates must contend with sudden changes in plans. They might be told at the last minute that they need to march an additional ten miles, or that they must reach a different destination. This is done to disorient candidates. As the candidates march up and down Pen-y-fan, a thirty-mile (forty-eight-kilometer) incline, instructors may appear and ask candidates to assemble a complicated foreign weapon or solve a difficult math problem. Candidates swim naked across icy rivers, carrying their weapons and clothes overhead.

These tests end with a forty-six-mile (seventy-four-kilometer) endurance march known as the Fan Dance. The Fan Dance must be completed in less than twenty hours, a time limit that means that most men must jog the distance, all while carrying fifty-five-pound bergens. There are no special allowances made for bad weather. Men get no extra supplies or time to finish the course. A few men have died trying to complete the Fan Dance in harsh, winter conditions.

Recruits reach the summit of Pen-y-fan, one of the final phases of selection for the SAS. Located in Brecon Beacons National Park, Pen-y-fan is the highest mountain in south Wales, reaching 2,907 feet (886 meters) above sea level.

The men who finish report to the SAS base in Hereford for fourteen weeks of additional training. Here, soldiers learn to operate weapons, work in four-man patrols, plan assaults, run missions behind enemy lines, gather intelligence, and conduct raids and acts of sabotage. They learn to move without being seen, to hide out in a meter-deep trench, and to survive combat. Candidates are put through the rigors of interrogation and learn how to function in different environments. Finally, the men undergo a four-week parachute course. After the successful completion of eight jumps, the candidates return to Hereford and receive their SAS badges.

5. Training and Equipment

The challenges of the SAS selection process are only the beginning for the SAS troopers. Once a candidate has been accepted, he undergoes rigorous training. If a soldier can't keep up the pace, he can be returned to his unit at any time. Some SAS training practices are so grueling that they cause public controversy. SAS officials argue that though their methods may seem extreme to outsiders, they are necessary to prepare SAS units for any and all possible situations.

The men who pass selection return to Hereford for an additional fourteen weeks of training. Every SAS squadron is divided into four sixteen-man specialist troops: boat, mountain, mobility, and free-fall. Those selected in the boat troop will be trained as frogmen in canoeing and small boat handling. Mountain troopers will specialize in winter warfare, including alpine climbing and skiing. Mobility troops will learn to handle gunned Land Rovers. Free-fall troops will specialize in high-altitude parachuting. Each troop will contain one or more men who have another specialty, for example, a foreign language or training in counterrevolutionary warfare.

Training for Real-Life Situations

During the initial phase of training, SAS troopers undergo many prisoner-of-war simulations, including capture, torture, and interrogation. In order to make the training real, the exercises can be brutal. A trooper may be beaten and blindfolded, and may undergo sensory deprivation. He may have a hood thrown over him, be left alone in a room for several hours, and suddenly hear the buzzing of power tools right by his head. He may be stripped naked, hosed with ice water, and left alone while he hears a frightening beating going on in the next room. These uncomfortable, frightening exercises are designed to force the trooper into breaking

Interrogation Training

"As I passed the corner of the outbuilding on my left, I saw the blur of black bala-clavas [a type of woolen hood] . . . Suddenly a group of four or five men roared onto the path and jumped on me . . . I landed with a thud on my back. One of them produced a rough Hessian sack, dragged it over my head and tied it securely around my neck . . . Having my sight removed was the worst part. I sensed I was being dragged down a long corridor . . . I was roughly pulled upright by a violent tug under the armpits. My arms were yanked behind my back and held in two less than delicate arm locks . . . there was a horrendous disorienting crackling noise seeping from every direction, as if every inch of the walls was conducting the sound of a badly tuned radio. Its pitch, frequency, and volume were unwavering. There was nothing in the white noise to focus on, but it was just loud enough to drown out normal conversation and disrupt your thinking."

—Sarah Ford, member of Det, an intelligence unit attached to the SAS, quoted in Stephen Bull's book, *SAS: Special Forces in Action*.

WHO DARES WINS

down and giving information. The rationale behind interrogation training is that with realistic training, soldiers will be better able to overcome fears of death, pain, and the unknown should prisoner-of-war situations occur.

When Jock Lewes trained the first SAS troopers, he exposed less-experienced soldiers to simulations of enemy fire. The SAS uses similar exercises today when training police bodyguards. Troopers outfitted with bullet-proof vests are made to stand in the path of bullets in order to experience the distinctive sounds of a rifle being fired at them.

The Uniform

The official SAS uniform includes a beige beret with a dark blue patch bearing the silver dagger and light blue winged insignia. A scroll beneath the insignia bears the official SAS motto: Who Dares Wins. Because the SAS usually operates in secret, these items are almost never worn in public or on active duty. SAS members often wear the uniforms or badges of other regiments, especially during counterinsurgency operations. Most often, SAS troopers wear lightweight, nondescript fatigues and wool pullovers and hats. The fatigues allow movement and protection from the elements. They are made of material that dries quickly with body heat.

This photo shows some of the equipment an SAS operative might use: (1) SAS regiment beret; (2) M16A2 rifle; (3) M203 40 mm grenade launcher *(attached to the M16A2)*; (4) army belt; (5) golok (a machete).

Finally, all SAS troopers have a good pair of boots at their disposal. Proper fit is important. Even a minor injury like a blister could slow a mission. A good fit will help a trooper avoid injuries and blisters, and firm support prevents sprains and fractures.

Equipment

Basic equipment often proves to be the most important equipment. Simple plastic bags, for example, are essential. They can be used to waterproof valuable equipment. They can also be used to store bodily waste, which left on the ground could alert an enemy to a soldier's presence. Basic items usually carried by an SAS trooper include a map, flashlight, compass, wire for making trip wires, fish line for assorted uses, survival knife, medical kit, dehydrated rations, ammunition, binoculars, matches, water purification tablets, and foreign currency. Troopers usually keep a sledgehammer and a pair of bolt cutters handy. Bolt cutters can be used to cut locks and chains. If these fail, the seven-pound sledge hammer can be used to break in just about anywhere. Teams may share bulkier items, such as cooking stoves, radios, eating utensils, and a water supply.

Unlike most other army units, the SAS are virtually free to choose their own weapons. Because troopers will likely need to operate in confined, crowded places, weapons must be short-barreled and accurate. Many SAS troopers carry a 12-gauge Remington Wingmaster shotgun. In addition to its capacity as a weapon, the Remington's short, solid shot blast is useful for blowing doors off their hinges. Once inside a terrorist area, SAS troopers often rely on short bursts from submachine guns such as the Heckler and Koch MP5 9 mm. Magnesium concussion grenades, or "flash bangs," are used to startle enemies. Tear gas is also favored by SAS troopers, who must then use gas masks so they aren't disabled by the gas themselves.

Special mission teams may need special equipment such as parachutes,

SAS paratroopers drop from low-flying planes onto water and land, often behind enemy lines.

diving equipment, and inflatable boats to support their operations. Various climates and terrain may also demand special equipment. If troops are operating in the jungle, they may require machetes, hammocks, insect repellent, foot powder, and antibacterial drugs. Soldiers working in the mountains might need skis, waterproof thermal clothing, snow shoes, and ice picks.

Rules of Conduct

SAS troopers are bound by a set of instructions known as Rules of Engagement. Every soldier is expected to know these rules by heart. In essence, the Rules of Engagement require that troops use minimum force and carry out no unnecessary killing. This means that troops are not to open fire unless they have been fired upon first or think beyond a reasonable doubt that innocent lives are at stake. These rules are designed to protect innocent bystanders from wild shooting and irresponsible gunplay.

The Present 6. and Future of the SAS

The very existence of the SAS—a military force that performs most operations in secret—may seem at odds with democratic society. But other Western military branches are evolving along the lines of the SAS. New threats demand new tactics. Over the past few years, military strategists in the Pentagon and elsewhere have urged military services to change the ways that they fight. The September 11, 2001, terror attacks on the Pentagon outside Washington, D.C., and the World Trade Center in New York City startled military forces. It became necessary to rethink standard methods of defense and combat.

SAS: Counterterrorist Specialists

Terrorists and guerrillas operate without warning and without apparent boundaries. Wars have moved from battlefields to shopping malls and city streets. It is hard to fight an enemy when one doesn't know who the enemy is, where they are located, or when they might attack. Ground forces need to develop intelligence to learn who the enemy is and why, where, and when they might attack. Some forces must be small enough to be dynamic. Well trained and aggressive, special forces operate best when they have the freedom to get a job done their own way. A successful, small, well-organized mission can also reduce the number of casualties during a conflict. These basic principles resemble those that shape U.S. Special Forces operations, such as those by the Army Green Berets, Navy Seals, Army Rangers, Delta Force Commando, and covert CIA operatives, as well as the SAS, around the world. Many in the military look to these groups to help define future military strategy.

Because individual members of the SAS cannot be named or identified publicly, the SAS seems shrouded in mystery. In photographs, faces of SAS troopers are blacked-out. The exact numbers of SAS soldiers are never disclosed. Their participation in any particular campaign is rarely made public. Anonymity is essential to SAS operations. Occasionally, politicians want the public to know about special forces operations. Other times, operations make their way into the press by accident, such as during the televised siege of the Iranian Embassy in 1980.

The SAS in Afghanistan

Currently, the SAS is in the public eye once more. Though the United Kingdom's Ministry of Defense never comments on the activities of its special forces, stories about their recent activities have made the papers. Britain is a close ally of the United States. It is presumed that two of the SAS's four squadrons assisted U.S. military operations in Afghanistan following the September 11, 2001, terrorist attacks. (One SAS squadron is always kept in Britain to counter possible terrorist threats at home.) It was reported that the SAS went behind enemy lines to gather intelligence that would help allied forces improve their targeting. They may have been called on to establish friendships with tribal forces in Afghanistan, helping them plan and execute operations against the Taliban, Afghanistan's Islamic fundamentalist government that gave refuge to Osama bin Laden. Bin Laden is the man widely believed to have planned and funded several terrorist attacks against the United States, including the attacks of September 11, 2001.

SAS members follow a U.S. Special Forces operative to an Al Qaeda training camp. Usually kept from the public eye, recent terrorist activity has forced many militaries to adjust their methods of fighting. Stealthy and aggressive, units such as the SAS are important resources in defending against terrorism.

It is likely that the SAS helped to track down other leaders of the Taliban and Al Qaeda, a worldwide network of Islamic terrorists that has declared a holy war against the United States.

Col. Terry Taylor of the International Institute for Strategic Studies told London's *Financial Times* that the special forces in Afghanistan were performing the types of operations for which they had been trained. "The only thing that has changed," he said, "is that their role is so public." One newspaper reported that SAS troopers and Delta Force

soldiers formed a forty-man team to search for Taliban and Al Qaeda leaders hiding in the Himalayan mountain range in Kashmir. Another reported that British and U.S. Special Forces were in secret training camps in the Afghan mountains, learning to navigate the rocky terrain on horses and motorbikes. One paper reported that SAS troops helped U.S. forces to kill 800 Taliban soldiers who were hiding in the mountains in eastern Afghanistan.

When Taliban prisoners in Mazar-e-Sharif revolted, TV news bulletins showed unidentified Western soldiers in desert camouflage and plain clothes fighting alongside Northern Alliance forces. Some of the plainclothes soldiers wore beards and Afghan dress. Some carried Kalashnikov rifles. Others carried rifles with laser scopes. Some people guessed that the Western soldiers were from the U.S. Army's Delta Force and Green Berets, and Great Britain's SAS. Because these soldiers work hard to keep their identities secret, they probably were not too happy to have their images televised.

A member of the SAS inspects a deserted Al Qaeda training camp in Afghanistan. After the terrorist attacks of September 11, 2001, the SAS teamed with U.S. Special Forces to fight terrorism.

Future Missions

Reportedly, U.S. president George W. Bush was so impressed with the SAS that he asked it to destroy Al Qaeda bases in remote regions of East Africa. The exact missions are being kept top secret. According to the London-based newspaper *News of the World*, SAS troopers must go into isolation before their departure. They live in an aircraft hangar and are kept away from other soldiers and civilians. Even the Royal Air Force pilots transporting the SAS troopers are not told where they are flying until they are already in flight.

Concerns about future terrorist attacks mean that the skills and service of Britain's elite troops, especially the SAS, are highly valued. The SAS is reportedly having trouble recruiting enough troopers to meet current demand. For the first time in its history, it is actively recruiting new applicants. According to the *London Times*, the SAS, which counts roughly 200 members at its full strength, needs 200 more troops to join the next round of selection tests. Each squadron of from 50 to 60 troops is currently about ten men short.

One reason that the SAS is short of men is simply because it is so difficult to qualify new recruits. Fewer than one in ten applicants pass the rigorous selection process. Another reason is that candidates can make more money working for private businesses. Some companies can offer men with SAS skills, training, and abilities more than the equivalent of $140,000 a year. The average SAS trooper earns about $35,000. "The general reason that people from security forces are popular is that they are very resourceful, self-disciplined and they have good communication skills," a representative for Armor Group Services told Britain's *Sunday Express*. Excellent training, aggressiveness, and the ability to make decisions under high stress are other reasons that SAS troopers are highly valued in the job market.

When the SAS was created, its purpose was to create terror behind enemy lines. Today, the SAS mainly prevents terror wherever it poses a threat, whether at home or abroad. With new threats arising in the Middle East, Africa, and Asia, it is likely that the SAS will be called to act in these regions. What they accomplish may come out in bits and pieces over time. A mission may be televised or reported in the newspaper. But whatever comes out in the press and in history books, it is likely that only a few SAS troopers ever will know the full story.

Glossary

abseil   A technique that uses ropes and pulls to navigate down steep surfaces, such as buildings and mountains; rappelling.

anorak   A heavy jacket with a hood.

autonomy   A self-governing state.

cache   A hiding place used to store provisions and valuables.

convoy   A group of vehicles that travels together for reasons of protection.

counterinsurgency   A political or military strategy intended to suppress a revolt.

guerrilla   A member of a small military unit that usually operates against its country's ruling government.

insignia   A badge of office or rank.

insurgency   A state of rebellion.

intelligence   Secret information.

junta   A group of military officers ruling a country after seizing power.

loyalist   One who maintains loyalty to an established government.

propaganda   Material given out by advocates of a particular cause.

reconnaissance   A mission to gather information, usually about the activities of an enemy or characteristics of a particular area.

regime   A form of government.

rendezvous   A meeting at a prearranged time and place.

resistance   An underground organization dedicated to liberating its country from military occupation.

territorial army   A group of local militia units raised to be called upon in times of national emergency.

terrorism   The unlawful use of violence by one group to intimidate another; such as bombings, kidnapping, and assassinations.

For More Information

Web Sites

Due to the changing nature of Internet links, the Rosen Publishing Group, Inc., has developed an online list of Web sites related to the subject of this book. This site is updated regularly. Please use this link to access the list:

http://www.rosenlinks.com/iso/sas/

For Further Reading

Brown, Ashley, ed. *The British 22nd SAS Regiment: Undercover Fighters.* New York: Villard Books, 1986.

Dickens, P. *SAS: The Jungle Frontier.* London: Arms and Armour Press, 1983.

Gander, Terry. *Encyclopaedia of the Modern British Army.* Cambridge, England: P. Stephens, 1981.

Ladd, James, and Keith Melton. *Clandestine Warfare: Weapons and Equipment of the SOE and OSS.* London: Blandford Press, 1988.

Niven, B. M. *Special Men, Special War: Portraits of the SAS and Dhofar.* Singapore: Imago Productions Pte. Ltd., 1990.

Secret Agent's Handbook: The WWII Spy Manual of Devices, Disguises, Gadgets, and Concealed Weapons. Guilford, CT: Lyons Press, 2001.

White, Terry. *The SAS Fighting Techniques Handbook.* New York: Lyons Press, 2001.

Bibliography

Bull, Stephen. *SAS: Special Forces in Action*. London: Publishing News Ltd., 2000.

Connor, Ken. *Ghosts: An Illustrated Story of the SAS*. London: Cassell & Co., 2000.

Davies, Barry. *The Complete Encyclopedia of the SAS*. London: Virgin Publishing, 1998.

Davies, Barry. *Heroes of the SAS*. London: Virgin Publishing, 2000.

Ford, Sarah. *One Up: A Woman in Action with the SAS*. London: Harper Collins, 1997.

George, Jackie, with Susan Ottaway. *She Who Dared: Covert Operations in Northern Ireland with the SAS*. Barnsley, England: Leo Cooper, 1999.

Geraghty, Tony. *This Is the SAS*. London: Arms and Armour Press, 1982.

Geraghty, Tony. *Who Dares Wins*. London: Arms and Armour Press, 1983.

Haswell, Jock. *The British Army: A Concise History*. London: Thames and Hudson, 1975.

Hoe, Alan. *David Stirling: The Authorised Biography of the Creator of the SAS*. London: Warner Books, 1994.

Hunter, Robin. *True Stories of the SAS*. London: Virgin Books, 1995.

Jeapes, T. *SAS: Operation Oman*. London: William Kimber, 1980.

Kemp, Anthony. *The SAS: Savage Wars of Peace 1947 to the Present*. London: Penguin Books Ltd., 2001.

Lewes, John. *Jock Lewes: Co-Founder of the SAS*. Barnsley, England: Leo Cooper, 2000.

Newsinger, John. *Dangerous Men: The SAS and Popular Culture*. London: Pluto Press, 1997.

Ramsay, Jack. *SAS: The Soldiers' Story*. London: Macmillan, 1996.

Rommel, Erwin, edited by B. H. Liddell Hart. *The Rommel Papers*. New York: Harcourt, Brace, 1953.

Short, J. G. *The Special Air Service*. London: Osprey Publishing, 1981.

Strawson, J. A. *A History of the SAS Regiment*. London: Secker & Warburg, 1984.

Thompson, Leroy. *SAS: Great Britain's Elite Special Air Service*. Osceola, WI: Motorbooks International, 1994.

Weale, Adrian. *The Real SAS*. London: Sidgwick & Jackson, 1998.

Index

A

Al Qaeda, 51, 53, 54

B

Barkworth, Eric, 24
bin Laden, Osama, 50
Brecon Beacons, Wales, 34, 36
Bull, Stephen, 37, 42

C

Calvert, Mike, 28
Churchill, Winston, 23
Clark, Dudley, 14
Commando Layforce, 12, 13

D

Davies, Barry, 35
de la Billiere, Peter, 33
Delta Force, 49, 51–53
Det, the (14th Intelligence Company), 29, 42
Diplomatic Protection Group, 6

F

Ford, Sarah, 29, 42

14th Intelligence Company (the Det), 29, 42

G

Galtiere, Leopoldo, 32
Green Berets, 49, 53

H

Harrison, Derrick, 20
Hereford, England, 26, 39, 40
Hitler, Adolf, 10, 20
Hussein, Saddam, 32

I

International Institute for Strategic Studies, 51
interrogation training, 41–43
Irish Republican Army (IRA), 30

L

L Detachment, 14
Lewes, Jock, 12–15, 16, 18–19, 43
  death of, 20
    SAS insignia/motto and, 20, 21
Lewes bomb (sticky bomb), 16, 20
Lock, Trevor, 5–6

Long Range Desert Group, 18–19

M
Malayan Emergency, 27–28
Mayne, Blair "Paddy," 21

N
NATO, 33

O
One Up: A Woman in Action with the SAS, 29
Operation Nimrod, 7–9
Operation STORM, 31

R
Rommel, Erwin, 14, 19, 21
Royal Air Force, 16, 35, 54
Rules of Engagement, 47

S
SAS
    in Afghanistan, 50–53
    equipment used by, 45–47
    in Falkland Islands, 32
    first operation of, 16–17
    future of, 54–55
    in Gulf War, 32–33
    insignia of, 21, 43
    in Malaya, 27–28, 34
    motto of, 21, 43
    in Northern Ireland, 29, 30–31
    in Oman, 31
    origins of, 12–17
    post–World War II, 24–26
    Rules of Engagement and, 47
    secrecy and, 26, 30–31, 43, 48, 49, 53

selection process for, 34–39, 40
selection tests, 36–38
split into two units, 21
training for, 39, 40–41
uniform of, 43–45
women in, 29
in World War II, 13–17, 18–23
SAS: Special Forces in Action, 37, 42
Scholey, Peter, 37
2nd SAS, 21, 22–23
sickeners, 37
Special Forces (United States), 49, 53
Special Raiding Squadron (SRS), 21, 22
Stirling, David, 12–15, 18–19, 23
    capture of, 21, 23
    SAS insignia/motto and, 21
Stirling, William, 21
Sukarno, President (Indonesia), 28

T
Taliban, 50–53
Taylor, Terry, 51
terrorist attacks
    Iranian Embassy (London, 1980), 5–9
    Munich Olympics (1972), 6–7
    World Trade Center and Pentagon (2001), 48, 50
Thatcher, Margaret, 32
These Men Are Dangerous, 19–20
21st SAS, 25, 28
22nd SAS, 26, 28, 34, 35

W
Who Dares Wins (SAS motto), 21, 43
Woodhouse, John, 34
World War II, 10–17, 18–23, 26, 28, 32
    after, 24–26

About the Author

Amanda Ferguson is a writer living in Los Angeles.

Credits

Cover, pp. 1, 4, 33, 51, 52 © AP/Wide World Photos; pp. 8, 11, 22, 25, 27 © Hulton/Archive/Getty Images; p. 12 © Imperial War Museum, London #E21340; p. 20 picture from the front cover of Jock Lewes, Co-Founder of the SAS © John Lewes; p. 31 © Maps.com/Corbis; pp. 39, 44 © Robin Adshead, The Military Picture Library/Corbis; p. 46 © Martin McKenzie, The Military Picture Library/Corbis.

Design and Layout

Les Kanturek

Editor

Christine Poolos